Why is the Sky blue?

compiled and written by
Geraldine Taylor

illustrated by
Amy Schimler

KT-176-755

700033033904

Who wakes the birds up in the morning?

Birds wake up by themselves as soon as it gets light. They like singing and finding food early.

What do birds say when they sing?

Male birds sing to attract female birds, and to warn other males to keep away.

How do baby birds get out of their eggs?

Do fish know who their parents are?

No, not like baby animals do. Some parent fish protect their babies, but most baby fish have to look after themselves.

Can fish hear things?

Yes, fish have ear parts. They can hear the vibrations of other fish and water creatures.

What are bees looking for?

Honeybees look inside flowers for sweet food called nectar. They make honey from this.

Why do flowers smell nice?

Is there anyone else just like me?

Why is the sky blue?

White sunlight is really made up of
many different colours mixed together.
The blue gets scattered everywhere into the
air, which makes the sky look blue to us.

Why do stars twinkle?

Starlight seems to twinkle as it ripples through Earth's moving air.

Why do trees lose their leaves?

In summer, leaves use the sun's energy to help the tree grow. In winter, trees rest. They don't need their leaves any more, so they fall off.

Do trees breathe?

Yes. Trees breathe in a gas called carbon dioxide through their leaves. They change this into the fresh air we breathe, called oxygen.

What do trees eat?

How do penguins keep warm?

Emperor penguins live in Antarctica, the coldest place in the world. They have waterproof feathers and fluffy down, and huddle together in big groups to keep warm.

How big are icebergs?

Icebergs can be as small as a tennis ball
or as large as a whole city.
Most of the iceberg is under the sea,
only the tip is above it.

If you enjoyed the Booktime edition of

Why is the sky blue?

you'll love these other Ladybird fact books:

Bugs

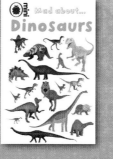

Dinosaurs

Ponies

Sharks

You could try sharing these books of rhymes:

BEDTIME RHYMES

NURSERY RHYMES

RHYMES TO SHARE

SINGALONG NURSERY RHYMES

Or reading these great stories:

The Three Billy Goats Gruff

Little Red Hen

Town Mouse and Country Mouse

The Gingerbread Man